P9-CEL-545

Valparaiso Public Library
103 Jefferson Street
Valparaiso, IN 46383

totally tolerant

Your Tolerance IQ

YOU PROBABLY LIKE TO THINK THAT YOU'RE A PRETTY BROAD-MINDED, TOLERANT PERSON. BUT HOW MUCH HAVE YOU THOUGHT ABOUT YOUR BIASES? TAKE THIS QUIZ TO SEE WHAT YOU KNOW ABOUT TOLERANCE.

True or False?

1 Tolerance is a new idea.

2 It's best to have friends who are a lot like you.

3 Everyone has some biases, or prejudices.

4 Bias often comes out in the language we use and the jokes we tell.

5 Teens cannot do very much to change the prejudice in the world.

Answer key:

(1) False. The idea of tolerance is hundreds of years old. Find out more in Chapter One. **(2)** False. "Sticking with your own kind" can be an example of intolerance. Read more in Chapter Two. **(3)** True. And it can be hard to be fully aware of all your prejudices. Find out more in Chapter Three. **(4)** True. Many of the words people use are more hurtful than they think. Check out Chapter Four to learn more. **(5)** False. Intolerance is a big problem, but your generation can tackle it! Chapter Five will show you how.

Chapter one: Hanaa's story appeared on tolerance.org. Used by permission. The information on pages 10–11 is from Mintel International, Chicago/U.S. Census Bureau, 2005. **Chapter three: Kevin's story** is excerpted from "Teased for Wearing a Turban," by Kevin Mangat, www.tolerance.org, April 14, 2005. Used by permission. **Karlee's story** is excerpted from "Homophobia in the Hallways," by Karlee Reid, www.tolerance.org, September 28, 2005. Used by permission. **Bob's story** was originally published in "What's a Bully?" by Denise Rinaldo, in *Scholastic Choices*, October 2001. **Molly's story** was originally published in "Rejected! Kids Who Don't Fit In," by Pearl Gaskins, in *Scholastic Choices*, November/December 1999. **Kristen's story** was originally published in "Decoding Dyslexia," by Sean McCollum, in *Scholastic Choices*, October 2006. **Giancarlo's and Massawa's stories** were originally published in "Poor in a Land of Plenty," by Denise Rinaldo, in *Scholastic Choices*, April/May 2005.

Except when noted by captions, the photos in this book are for illustration purposes only and do not depict the real people profiled in the book.

Photographs © 2008: age fotostock: 80 (Brand X Pictures), 64 (ImageSource), 82 top (PhotoAlto), 40 (Pixland); Corbis Images: 33 (Alexander Benz/zefa), 39 (Bettmann), 20, 27 (Vernon Bryant/Dallas Morning News), 48 (Patrick Giardino), 77 (JLP/Sylvia Torres/zefa), 100 bottom (Rob Lewine/zefa), 69 (Lucidio Studio Inc.), 95 (Will & Deni McIntyre), 45 (Chuck Savage), 63 (Turbo/zefa), 37 inset (Visuals Unlimited); Getty Images: 100 top (Ewa Ahlin), 81 (Paul & Lindamarie Ambrose), 10 (Kevin Cooley), cover center left (Paul Costello), 61 (Andy Crawford), 65 (Robert Daly), 88 (Digital Vision), 86 (Erik Dreyer), 98 (F64), 30 (Chris Graythen), 58 (Holly Harris), 42 (Hulton Archive), cover center, back cover top (Hummer), 68 (Image Source Bank), 66 (Michael Lander), 17 (Sarah Leen), 101 bottom (Eri Morita), 91 (Hans Neleman), cover bottom right (White Packert), cover center right (Barbara Penoyar), 84, 85 (David Pfeifroth), 83 (David Samuel Robbins), 101 top (SD Productions), 74 (Margo Silver), cover top left (Julia Smith), 92 (Steve Smith), 103 (Jeff Speed), 15 (SW Productions), cover top right, back cover bottom (Ulrik Tofte), 5, 76 (Rachel Watson); iStockphoto: 73 (dra_schwartz), back cover center, cover top center (Scott Griessel), cover bottom left (Tina Lorien); JupiterImages: 90 (BananaStock), 96 (Comstock Images), 72 (Image Source), 94 (Polka Dot Images), 67 (Michael Siluk), 37 main (Chip Simons); NEWSCOM/Chris Graythen: 23; PhotoEdit: 35 (Spencer Grant), 54 (Robin Nelson), 82 bottom (Michael Newman), 14 (David Young-Wolff); ShutterStock, Inc./David Davis: 78; Superstock, Inc./Stockbyte: 25; The Granger Collection, New York: 18; The Image Works/John Birdsall: 4, 6, 8.

Cover design: Marie O'Neill
Book production: The Design Lab
CHOICES editor: Bob Hugel

Library of Congress Cataloging-in-Publication Data
Webber, Diane, 1968–
 Totally tolerant: spotting and stopping prejudice / Diane Webber and Laurie Mandel.
    p. cm.
Includes bibliographical references and index.
ISBN-13: 978-0-531-13867-0 (lib. bdg.)   978-0-531-20525-9 (pbk.)
ISBN-10: 0-531-13867-4 (lib. bdg.)   0-531-20525-8 (pbk.)
1. Prejudices. 2. Toleration. I. Mandel, Laurie, 1963– II. Title.
 HM1091.W43 2009
 303.3'85—dc22   2007051873

No part of this publication may be reproduced in whole or in part, or stored in a retrieval system, or transmitted in any form or by any means, electronic, mechanical, photocopying, recording, or otherwise, without written permission of the publisher. For information regarding permission, write to Scholastic Inc., 557 Broadway, New York, NY 10012.

© 2008 Scholastic Inc.
All rights reserved. Published in 2008 by Franklin Watts, an imprint of Scholastic Inc. Published simultaneously in Canada. Printed in the United States of America. SCHOLASTIC, FRANKLIN WATTS, and associated logos are trademarks and/or registered trademarks of Scholastic Inc.

1 2 3 4 5 6 7 8 9 10 R 17 16 15 14 13 12 11 10 09 08

SCHOLASTIC CHOICES

Spotting and
stopping
prejudice

totally

tolerant

PORTER COUNTY LIBRARY

Diane Webber and Laurie Mandel

Valparaiso Public Library
103 Jefferson Street
Valparaiso, IN 46383

Franklin Watts®

J NF   303.385 WEB   VAL
Webber, Diane 1968-
Totally tolerant : spotting an
33410010181628

DISCARDED

aiso - Porter County
MAR 1 0 2009

totally tolerant

"COOL TO BE DIFFERENT"

Hanaa knew that Gibson High School (not the real name) in Richland, Washington, was very special. "It was a place where it was considered cool to be different," Hanaa says. Students at Gibson are Indian, Chinese, Cuban, Pakistani, and Indonesian, among other ethnicities. They try to appreciate and celebrate each other's backgrounds.

In seventh grade at Gibson, Hanaa started visiting her friends' homes during Christmastime to learn more about Christianity and the holiday. In turn, she taught her friends about the Islamic holy month of Ramadan. During Ramadan, Muslims fast, meaning they do not eat, from sunup until sundown. "I explained that I appreciated the humility and empathy fasting brings to a person," Hanaa writes on tolerance.org. "Molly, my punk/hippie friend, asked whether I would like it if she fasted with me to try and experience what I meant, despite the fact that she was not a Muslim. Immediately my face lit up—I had always wanted to have someone my own age fast with me."

Molly fasted with Hanaa every year until they graduated. Other friends would fast a few days out of the month with them. And a big group came to Hanaa's house every year for Eid al-Fitr, the feast at the end of Ramadan. "I appreciated that they were not only trying to understand the meaning of Ramadan," Hanaa says, "but that they were trying to understand what it was like to be me."

Today, Hanaa is a young adult. "I have never personally felt outcast or discriminated against," Hanaa says. "However, I have never felt as comfortable in being Muslim or Arab as I did when I was at Gibson. I wish I could re-create that sort of environment everywhere."

According to Hanaa, Gibson High School is a model of **tolerance**. Tolerance can be defined as respect for **diversity**. But those three terms—diversity, respect, and tolerance—are pretty abstract. So let's take a closer look at them.

DIVERSITY
RESPECT
TOLERANCE

Defining Diversity

Diversity means difference. You could talk about a diverse selection of apples in the supermarket, and you'd mean that there were a lot of different kinds to choose from. But people usually aren't talking about apples when they use the word. Diversity usually refers to a community of differing races, ethnicities, economic levels, sexual orientations, and physical abilities. Diversity means a mixture of people. If a group lacks diversity, it is **homogeneous**, which means "all the same."

IN THE MIX

How racially and ethnically diverse are U.S. teens? Have a look. There are approximately 26 million people between the ages of 12 and 17 living in the United States. This chart shows the racial and ethnic makeup of U.S. teens.

Other
<4%

Asian
<4%

Black or African American
16%

HISPANIC
17%

WHITE
60%

Spelling Out Respect

Respect has to do with having consideration for someone. It requires taking him or her seriously. Respect is refusing to insult people. Respect is resisting the temptation to gossip. Respect is not laughing at jokes that repeat **stereotypes**.

When someone asks for your respect, that person essentially means, "Listen to me." Often, that's not easy. But when you're really listening to people who are different from you—the way Hanaa and her friends listened to each other—then chances are you're respecting them, too.

Respecting diversity doesn't mean that you have to adopt the same beliefs as the next person. Molly didn't become a Muslim after fasting with Hanaa. But it does mean that you should try to understand and value the other person's beliefs.

Respecting diversity doesn't mean that you have to adopt the same beliefs as the next person.

SHOWING
respect

Here are some other ways to show respect.

RESPECT means looking at each person as a distinct individual. It means setting aside your prior ideas about who you think a person *should be* and seeing, instead, who that person *is*.

RESPECT means putting yourself in another person's shoes and doing your best to see things from that person's perspective.

RESPECT means not telling—or laughing at— insensitive jokes that make fun of whole groups of people.

RESPECT means saying hello to people who aren't in your group of friends.

RESPECT means keeping your word and doing what you promised.

RESPECT means telling bullies they're not funny.

RESPECT means reaching outside yourself and finding what you can learn from someone new.

"Find out what you can learn from someone new."

JOURNAL **IT!**

How have you shown respect for someone in the past week? If you can't think of a good example, brainstorm some ways that you can show respect to your friends and family today.

Here are some suggestions:

LISTEN to what your friends have to say; don't interrupt.

LOOK your parent in the eye when you talk with him or her.

If someone prepares you a meal, **REMEMBER** to say thank you.

OFFER to help a younger sibling with homework.

TALK in calm tones; don't yell.

Talking About Tolerance

The dictionary defines the term *tolerance* as "recognition of and respect for the opinions, practices, and behaviors of others." It is respect for diversity. But that's just the starting point. Tolerance has come to refer to a philosophy about how people can get along in their families, their communities, their countries, and the world.

Tolerance has to do with having respect for everyone's religion, gender, race, **ethnicity**, **sexual orientation**, and social class. Tolerance is an active process. It's not just about *accepting* other people's differences; it's about *respecting* these differences. That takes work. It also takes education.

tol·er·ance:

recognition of and respect for the opinions, practices, and behaviors of others

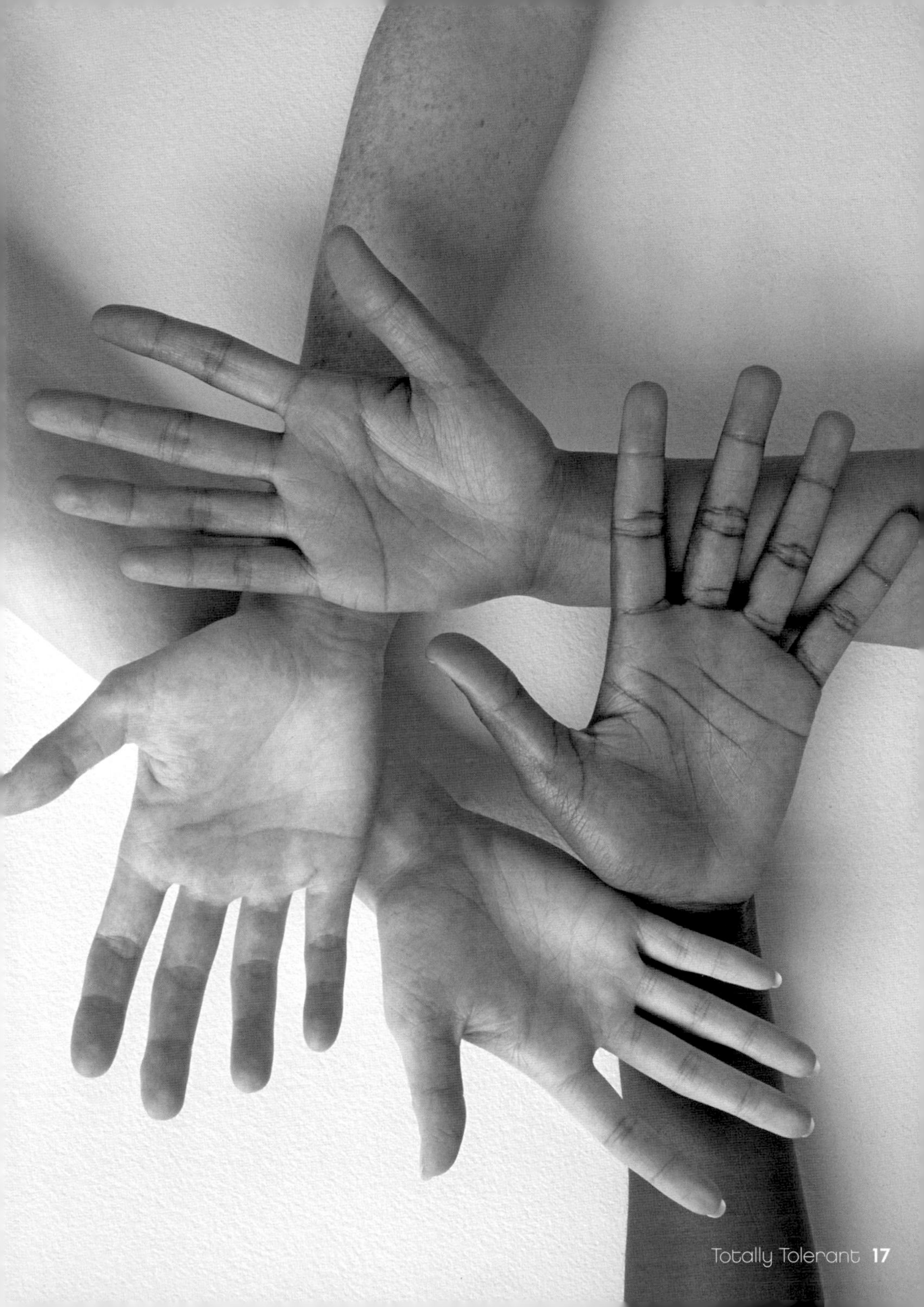

A History of Tolerance

Tolerance is not a new idea. In fact, the concept of tolerance has been around since the beginning of the history of the United States. When the American colonists split from Great Britain in the late 1700s, they worked the idea of tolerance into the new country's Bill of Rights. The document's First Amendment makes it clear that the government has to tolerate the citizens' rights to worship, speak, and protest: "Congress shall make no law respecting an establishment of religion . . . or abridging the freedom of speech, or of the press; or the right of the people peaceably to assemble. . . ."

At the time, the definition of *citizen* did not include many groups of people such as Native

"Harmony in Difference"

WHAT IS TOLERANCE ON A GLOBAL SCALE?
According to UNESCO (the United Nations Educational, Scientific, and Cultural Organization), "tolerance is respect, acceptance, and appreciation of the rich diversity of our world's cultures, our forms of expression, and ways of being human. Tolerance is harmony in difference."

Americans, enslaved peoples, and women. However, over time, more members of American society gained protection under these constitutional rights.

Today, tolerance of others continues to be crucial to the health of modern societies. In the United States, for example, most people are immigrants or descendants of immigrants. That means Americans come from a lot of different backgrounds—with different religions, different cultures, different skin colors, different abilities, different incomes. Tolerance is necessary for Americans to live together peacefully and happily.

totally
intolerant

THE STORY OF THE JENA 6

Jena is a town of just 3,000 people in Louisiana. Its population is 75 percent white and 12 percent African American. Before the autumn of 2006, few white residents of Jena saw it as an intolerant place.

But the experience of six African American teenagers there changed that.

The story of the Jena 6 began at an assembly at Jena High School on August 31, 2006. An African American student called out a question to then-principal Scott Windham: "Can I sit under the white tree?"

There was one big tree on campus that students could gather under to get out of the sun. To the African American students, it was known as "the white tree" because that is who usually sat there. Windham said, "Sit wherever you want." (He later said that he considered both the student's question and his answer jokes.)

The next day, there were three hangman's nooses hanging from the tree. Nooses are symbols of lynchings. Lynch mobs murdered thousands of African Americans between the years 1882 and 1968. The noose recalls these decades of terror in the United States. It was a time when African Americans could be murdered by a mob—usually with no consequences for the murderers.

"Can I sit under the white tree?"

This tree on the Jena High School campus was considered a place where only white kids could hang out.

Violence Erupts

Three white students were found to be responsible for the nooses. At first, expulsion was considered. But a discipline committee rejected it as too harsh. Instead, the students were sent to an alternative school for nine days. Then they served an in-school suspension for two weeks. School officials called the nooses a prank. No criminal complaint was filed.

But tensions were high between the white and African American students of the small town. There were several fights over the next few weeks. The principal called on Louisiana District Attorney Reed Walters to address students about the fights. But African American students say he referred to the nooses as an "innocent prank," which only made people angrier. African American students were also denied the opportunity to speak to the school board about the noose incident, because the board considered the matter settled.

On November 30, 2006, an arsonist set the school on fire. That crime remains unsolved.

Then, on December 4, 2006, six male African American students allegedly ambushed a white student, kicking and stomping him after he was unconscious. This time, police were called, and

Jena, LA
A small American town

Jena is a small town in central Louisiana. Approximately 3,000 people call it home. White residents make up about 75 percent of the town's total population and African Americans make up about 12 percent.

the six students were charged with attempted murder. Their shoes were considered deadly weapons.

The students' attack was clearly very wrong, but was this attempted murder? The white victim was treated at a local hospital and released. He attended a class-ring ceremony that night. Meanwhile, all of his alleged attackers faced adult charges that could put them in prison for as many as 30 years.

Jena, LA

Peaceful Protest

Word about what was happening in Jena spread gradually on the radio, Internet, and at colleges. People were outraged by how these six teenagers were being treated by the legal system.

A spotlight began to shine on the case, and protesters called on the district attorney to drop the charges. He did reduce them to battery and conspiracy charges. But the Jena 6, as the young men came to be known, still faced penalties of 15 to 20 years in prison.

On September 20, 2007, between 10,000 and 20,000 people came to Jena from all over the country in buses for a peaceful protest march. Many of them were college students.

"The students are my age," Maya Foster, 17, told the *Washington Post*. "It really hit home, because I think about that it could have been one of my classmates." Foster joined hundreds of high school students in a march through her neighborhood in Washington, D.C., in support of the Jena 6. There were similar marches in Philadelphia, Atlanta, and Detroit.

Jesse Jackson led one of the marches in support of the Jena 6.

The Case and the Aftermath

In Jena, school officials cut down the controversial "white tree." But they said it was part of a planned renovation of the school and unrelated to the case. Town officials have put together a committee of white, African American, and other community leaders to try to start talking more about racial issues and to repair the town's image.

Issues
of intolerance

The town of Jena and, indeed, the country as a whole face a lot of tough questions about race and tolerance in the aftermath of this incident.

WHY did African American students feel like they were not allowed to sit in a certain place on campus?

WHY was a student's question about the tree treated as a joke?

WHY weren't the nooses seen as a threat against the school's African American students? Didn't the school administrators know the history of lynching?

WHY did some students resort to violence?

WHY are African American males so likely to face maximum charges and maximum penalties if they enter the justice system?

check
yourself

Do any of the issues raised by the Jena 6 case hit home for you? Intolerance in your own community can be less obvious than you might expect. How does your school compare to Jena High School?

Are there places in your school that are "off limits" to one group or another based on race or some other aspect of identity?

Have you heard or made a biased remark and then tried to laugh it off?

This young woman was among the thousands of people who gathered for a civil rights march in Jena in September 2007.

FREE THE JENA SIX
JUSTICE FOR ALL

People are talking, thinking, and working out answers to all these questions. That is a positive outcome of the Jena 6 incident. Sadly, there's been a very negative outcome, too. Hundreds of racist vandals hung nooses in apparent copycat crimes all over the country. This powerful symbol of hate and **intolerance** appeared at the University of Maryland, Columbia University, and dozens of workplaces.

What can we do about it? One answer is to keep talking and learning about the history of **racism** and the power it still exerts today.

"Silence is not the answer," Beverly Daniel Tatum wrote in an opinion column in the *Washington Post*. Tatum is the president of Spelman College, a historically black college. In Jena, she sees missed opportunities for these difficult, important conversations—and dire consequences. "In the absence of dialogue, violence erupted," she wrote. "The school burned, multiple fights broke out, whites and blacks were injured, and the lives of six young black men were placed in limbo." She concludes, "In the end, the tree—the source of shade and the symbol of separation—was cut down. Now there is no refuge for anyone."

Talking About Intolerance

In Jena, we see the effects of one kind of intolerance—racism. It has been devastating to the town and many of its residents. But what, exactly, is intolerance? Intolerance is the lack of respect for diversity. It has to do with acting on a **prejudice**. Prejudice is a negative opinion that you hold before you even know anything about a person or situation.

Another word for prejudice is **bias**. That's a preference or idea that gets in the way of forming a fair judgment. You might have a bias against vegetables, for example, because you haven't yet found one that you like. This bias could keep you from ever trying another vegetable—so you would be keeping yourself ignorant about vegetables.

prejudice is BIAS

A bias against vegetables only hurts you (and maybe your grocery store), but a bias against groups of people has the potential to hurt you and any member of those groups you ever encounter. If a judge or jury is biased against a young African American man, does that man stand a chance of receiving a fair trial? This is the question at the heart of the Jena 6 case. And it is a question that has implications in courtrooms throughout the country.

Intolerance is the "you are NOT okay" impulse. It is looking at another group and judging it not only different, but also bad and wrong. There is a range of intolerance. In some schools, things are not so bad. Perhaps people of different ethnic groups get along in classrooms, but don't socialize outside of them. There may not be strong friendships, like Molly and Hanaa's in Chapter One, but there also is no violence.

In other communities, intolerance is dangerous. Hateful thoughts can become hurtful words, actions, and violence. Intolerance is a root cause of much of the pain and injustice in the world.

What Does Intolerance Lead To?

Different styles of dress, different ways of speaking, different foods to eat—all of these things can set people apart from one another. If we don't seek to understand these things, it is easy to be fearful of them. We might just find the differences odd and leave it at that. Or we might be offended by these differences and start to hate. Those who become consumed with hatred for people they don't understand can become destructive and even violent.

Here's a look at some of the destructive forms of intolerance.

Bullying

Bullies often try to exert power over someone who is perceived as different from the rest of the group. The person may be different because of his ethnicity or his size or his economic status—almost anything that could set him apart. The bully takes advantage of this person's "otherness" to intimidate and humiliate his target.

Intolerance from the rest of the group is what allows a bully to isolate a target. If everybody thinks, "Well, yeah, Tommy does dress funny," they'll be more likely to look away when Tommy becomes the butt of a bully's joke.

Demeaning Speech

Demeaning speech is another result of intolerance. In 2007, a radio talk show host demeaned the accomplishments of a winning women's college basketball team with racist, **sexist** language. He was fired.

The "n-word" in particular has an ugly history. It has been used to dehumanize and intimidate African Americans for hundreds of years. Though the word is often used casually now, many African American leaders argue that it should be taken out of our vocabulary. In fact, the NAACP (National Association for the Advancement of Colored People) held a funeral for the n-word in 2007, arguing that it should be laid to rest forever.

Bias Incidents

According to tolerance.org, a bias incident is conduct, speech, or expression that is motivated by bias or prejudice but is not a criminal act. The nooses hung from the tree in Jena were considered a bias incident rather than a **hate crime**, under the laws of the state. Bias incidents often violate the rules of a school, however, so its administrators may discipline students involved in bias incidents.

Hate Crimes

Hate crimes are attacks or threats made against people because of their race, ethnicity, national origin, religion, sexual orientation, or disability. Hate crimes are an attempt to terrorize whole groups of people, not just the individual victim. The FBI tracks hate crimes, and it says that under 10,000 hate crimes occur most years. But experts at the Southern Poverty Law Center disagree. They monitor hate groups in the United States. They believe that hate crimes are underreported and that the actual yearly total is closer to 191,000.

Some experts believe that as many as 191,000 hate crimes occur most years.

Think about it!

Have you ever experienced a form of intolerance? Has someone been biased against you? Have you been biased against someone else?

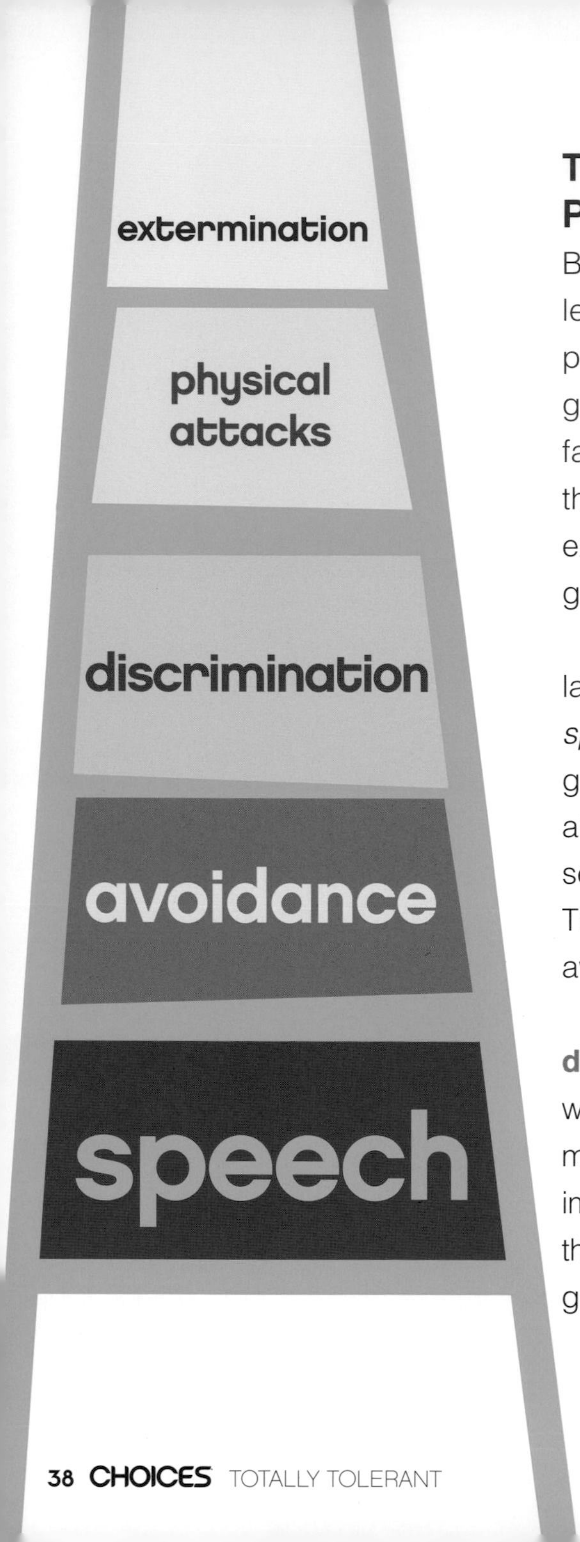

The Ladder of Prejudice

Bias and intolerance lead to violence in a predictable way. This graphic shows just how far prejudice can go—all the way to genocide, the extermination of an entire group of people.

The first rung on the ladder of prejudice is *speech*. That's when one group starts talking badly about another group. The second rung is *avoidance*. The groups begin staying away from each other.

The third step is **discrimination**. That's when one group—the more powerful one—imposes rules or laws that are unfair to the other group.

extermination

physical attacks

discrimination

avoidance

speech

The next rung is even worse. This is when the powerful group uses *physical attacks*, or violence against the other group. From there, the next step is *extermination*—the attempt to totally wipe out that other group.

A Jewish family being forced from their home during World War II

There are many examples of this progression in history. For example, before and during World War II, a political party in Germany called the Nazis launched a campaign of hateful speech against Jews. They then passed laws that discriminated against these fellow Germans. Later, Jews were attacked and their property was seized. Eventually, the Nazis tried to exterminate this group— and killed at least six million Jews in Europe.

We've learned that intolerance can become deadly. It is also much too common. Some of the effects of intolerance are dramatic and catch the attention of the whole world. But intolerance has an everyday face, too. It will sneak into many of our interactions if we aren't on the lookout for it. In the next chapter, we'll hear from students who have been on the receiving end of intolerance and bias in their daily lives.

real teens real stories

REAL INTOLERANCE

What are the ways that people are intolerant of one another? There are at least nine common types of bias—bias against race, religion, ethnicity, sexual orientation, gender, social affiliation, ability, appearance, and social class.

So how does intolerance feel? Real teens who have experienced it answered that question.

This photo of a store marked "White Only" was taken around 1950.

Bias #1: Race

Race is defined as "one of the major groups into which human beings can be divided. People of the same race usually share similar physical characteristics."

One of the most dangerous currents running through our society is racism. That's when people are prejudged, hated, or discriminated against because of their race.

Although freedom of religion was one of the founding values of the United States, the country does not have a history of freedom when it comes to race. Slavery was legal when the country was founded. Native Americans were forcibly removed from their lands. And as recently as the 1960s, African Americans—by law—had to drink at separate water fountains in many states.

Problems of racial discrimination persist today. Minority groups encounter racial discrimination in housing, education, the legal system, and the workplace. Racial discrimination is the most frequently filed charge with the federal Equal Employment Opportunity Commission.

Chrystal's Story

Chrystal, 14, is of mixed race. She is also one of the few students of color in a mostly white school in Long Island, New York. Chrystal reports:

My mom is from London, and my dad is from Nigeria. Everyone expects me to be like other black kids in our school—all ghetto and gangsta.

I'm not going to try to act like something that I'm not. I wasn't raised that way. Kids expect that of me because it's the image they see on TV. My friends will say to me, "You're so white," even though I'm quite dark-skinned. If my friend says that, I can kind of deal with it. But from people who think they're my friends but they're really not, it gets irritating and annoying.

People expect black teens to be not as smart, to get into trouble a lot. I'm not any of that. I'm really smart. I'm on committees. I'm in the National Junior Honor Society and the Global Language Honor Society. I've chosen to strive for the highest I could go and to be the best I can be.

Evan's Story

Evan* is an eighth grader, and like Chrystal, he knows people at his school who seem disappointed that he doesn't fit into his racial stereotype.

"I'm Asian and everyone assumes that I must be good in science and math and that I play the violin," says Evan. "It's not even true. I'm not very good in math. Even a teacher said to me, 'How can you be bad in math when you're Asian?'"

Even though these stereotypes are positive, Evan knows that they keep people from seeing who he *really* is. Says Evan: "It's all these assumptions that fabricate our identity for us about how we're supposed to be or act. And when you're not that, you feel like you don't fit in anywhere."

This student's name has been changed.

Bias #2: Religion

A religion is a specific system of belief, faith, and worship. Throughout history, there have been countless clashes over religion. And these conflicts continue today. People may hold biases against someone who is very religious, and others are biased against someone who has no religion.

People who are members of less-common religions in the United States, such as Judaism and Islam, may encounter bias as well. Muslim people saw a rise in bias against them after the terrorist attacks on September 11, 2001. The terrorists were Muslim, but by no means did they represent the Muslim people. And even today, Jewish people are targeted by neo-Nazi hate groups with alarming regularity.

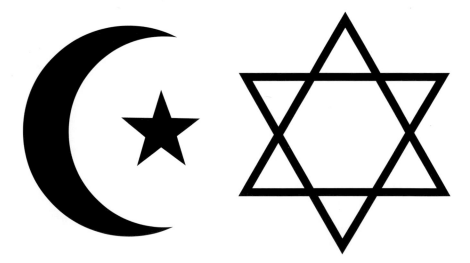

Kevin's Story

Kevin, 14, is a practicing Sikh. He follows his religion by wearing a turban and not cutting his hair. How would you feel if, by following your religion, you looked totally different from your classmates and even some of your relatives? Kevin wrote this essay about being teased for tolerance.org.

My religion is Sikh, and I am not allowed to cut any hair on my body for my whole life. We as Sikhs believe the hair on the body is a gift from Vāhigurū, the god we worship.

Nobody should be teased for following their religion, whether they are Sikh, Christian, or any other religion. Everybody knows that America is a country based on freedom, independence and formed by people from other countries and religions. So why does everybody still judge other people for having different skin color even though they are the ones who make up America?

When my school's basketball team met with our rival school to duke it out on the basketball court, I saw something unusual. I saw a boy wearing a turban. He wasn't alone or being treated differently just for wearing a turban or having a different color skin than the majority of his peers. He was being treated like any other student at his school.

You would think that my own teammates would also step up and act appropriately—mature and non-bigoted—like the members of the other team. I thought so, too. But when my team and I sat down, one of my so-called friends, someone I respected, made a joke about how this kid who was wearing a turban looked like my twin brother.

When I told my friend how I envy that kid for following his religion no matter what the cost, everybody on my team chuckled. I asked why they were chuckling and they told me that was the "lamest" thing I had ever said. They laughed even harder when they realized I was actually very serious.

Inspired by the kid wearing the turban, I told my friends that when they make fun of those following the Sikh religion, they are making fun of all other people for following their religions. Hearing this finally made them realize how much it hurts to be judged and how it feels to be a victim of bigotry.

Everyone should at least make an attempt to stop bigotry, even if it is not your own religion you are defending. By not doing so, you watch other people suffer just because you don't have the guts to stand up for what you believe in—freedom. Freedom from not being judged for how you look, dress, talk, or behave. It's better to be judged for who you are as a person.

Bias #3: Ethnicity

An ethnic group is a group of people who share the same national origins, language, or culture. This category can be a bit confusing because each group might have many subgroups. "Hispanic" is considered an ethnicity, but Hispanic people may come from Central America, South America, or the Caribbean. Ethnic bias comes in when all members of an ethnicity are expected to behave the same way. If you jump to conclusions about a person because of his or her ethnicity, that's an ethnic bias.

Gabi's Story

Gabi, 12, experienced bias from someone within her own ethnic group.

My mom is Puerto Rican and Jewish, and my dad is Italian and Christian. I have a Puerto Rican flag on my backpack and this boy started saying, "You can't be Jewish and Puerto Rican" because I have light skin. He's darker skinned, and it's obvious he's proud of his heritage. But he won't let me be Puerto Rican. He can't fathom that I'm Puerto Rican because I'm white.

He can't tell someone her race. It's like me telling you that you can't wear red and that's that! It makes no sense!

Imani's Story

Imani, 14, has a rich ethnic background. She was born in France and has ancestors from Iran and India. Today, she attends middle school in Long Island, New York, where she is one of only two Iranian students in the school. She has faced ethnic bias for a long time.

"When I moved here from France in first grade, a lot of kids were mean to me," says Imani. "They thought I was stupid because I didn't speak much English. They thought I didn't understand, so kids stayed away from me. I had no friends."

It was difficult for her as a little girl. "I'd come home and be really sad. But I got used to it," she says. "Now I feel I fit in better. People admire me because I speak English fluently. I also speak Persian."

Today, Imani's group of friends includes other kids who are members of different minority ethnic groups—Hispanic kids, Asian kids, Muslim kids. "I feel accepted," she says. "We understand each other."

Bias #4: Sexual Orientation

Sexual orientation refers to whether you are straight, gay, transgender (meaning a person identifies with the opposite gender), or bisexual (meaning a person is attracted to people of both genders). Gay teens face *a lot* of bias and harassment. More than 30 percent of gay youth were threatened or injured at school in 2001 alone.

More than 30 percent of gay youth were threatened or injured at school in 2001 alone.

30%

Karlee's Story

Karlee, 16, is a lesbian. She and her girlfriend have been frequently harassed at their high school. This is an excerpt of an essay she wrote for tolerance.org:

It has been impossible to count the number of times our learning environment was disrupted because of our sexuality. We do not feel we need to disguise our affection for each other. While I understand public displays of affection by homosexuals and heterosexuals are frowned upon, holding my girlfriend's hand should not in any way, shape, or form cause the student body to harass us for days on end.

While hallway harassment in school is bad enough, it's not the limit. We also have endured offensive e-mails, phone calls, harassment in the street, in the malls and other public places.

I was openly insulted by a group of classmates in one particular class. . . . I certainly did my best to ignore them—as did the teacher. On other occasions, when a student was being harassed that same teacher would put a stop to it immediately.

Zach's Story

Zach is a 16-year-old from a small town in Virginia. He's gay and president of the Gay-Straight Alliance (GSA) in his high school. That's a group for gay and straight kids to get together "for a discussion, a movie, or just to socialize," Zach explains.

He recalls a disturbing incident last year. "The GSA put up some posters encouraging people to come to our meetings," Zach says, "and on one of them someone scrawled [a derogatory term] all over, then proceeded to rip it." Since then, posters for the group have been torn down.

Still, for the most part, Zach says his school is a fairly tolerant place. "I would just like to assert the importance of Gay Straight Alliances," he says. "I remember being very lost in middle school, with nowhere to really turn. It feels good to be around other people who share the same fundamental values of tolerance, acceptance, and love."

Bias #5: Gender

Gender refers to being male or female—but that's not all. It also refers to all the expectations we have for what it means to be a girl or a boy in our culture. Gender stereotypes and bias can lock people into roles that are limiting. "Girls aren't good at math" and "Boys don't cry" are examples of gender bias.

Lana's Story

Lana*, 15, has to deal with gender bias at home from her father.

My dad is against women in general. He doesn't say the same things to my brother as he does to my mom or me. He'll say things like, "you're worthless and disgusting." He's never said anything to my brother. It's not right that he says it at all. He doesn't let my mom work, so she doesn't make any money. He berates her and makes her feel empty. It's become normal to her.

I see all of this. I have a strong center. I feel it. It's not okay to let people berate you or make you feel you can't do something. Once you do that, you give away everything you have. Because of this I'm stronger and it has shaped me to be who I am today: strong, aware, and determined.

*This student's name has been changed.

Bob's Story

Being a boy can be rough as well. Bob Fishel, now 17, was victimized by bullies during his seventh- and eighth-grade years.

It's hard to describe how being bullied felt because any one thing alone wouldn't have been a big deal. But when it happens every day, it starts to make you crazy.

There were so many little things. Pushing me for no reason, slamming my locker shut if I was getting something from it, or knocking stuff off my tray in the cafeteria. People did it all to me.

A couple of times, the bullying just got to me and I lashed out. It happened one time in shop class, which was always horrible for me. I wasn't very good at shop.

I was waiting to get a turn with a brush and finally got one. Then one of the guys in class just grabbed the brush from me. I was so angry. I'd been waiting forever. He was just like, "It's not your turn. You're not good enough."

What I would usually do is bottle up my feelings and not say anything. But this time, I couldn't. I took a swing at the guy and he moved. I hit one of the shop vents and a horrible pain shot through my arm. My hand was broken.

What happened in shop class that day was typical of how most kids would act when somebody was bullying me. They'd either ignore it or join in.

Bias #6: Social Affiliation

"Social affiliation" refers to the groups you join. In high schools, social affiliation bias might play out between the jocks and the brainiacs, or between the popular kids and the outcasts. If you've had nasty thoughts about people you don't really know—just because of who their friends are—that's social affiliation bias.

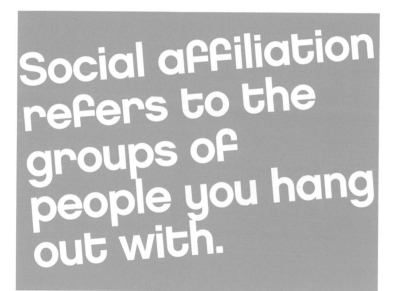

Social affiliation refers to the groups of people you hang out with.

Molly's Story

Molly couldn't wait for the weekends. At her high school in a suburb of Seattle, Washington, she suffered multiple humiliations every day. "I'd ask a question, and people would say 'I don't know' or they'd turn their backs on me," says Molly, now 17. "I got spit on several times."

If Molly, whose tastes run to black clothes and Goth styles, ventured into the cafeteria, she risked having kids yell comments like "freak!" or throw french fries or trash her way. So she avoided the lunchroom. "I just kept my head down," she says, "I hunched over, and I walked."

She admits, "After a while, it starts to wear you down. I couldn't sleep. I got sick a lot. I got really depressed for a while." Molly wound up turning to her doctor, who prescribed antidepressants. "Kids who do the harassing say 'it's all in good fun'," Molly says. "It's not all in good fun."

Bias #7: Ability

Ability refers to what a person can do. Everyone has different strengths and weaknesses. A person who gets teased and ridiculed because he is not a good athlete has experienced ability bias. Ability bias can be especially hurtful and damaging for people who have serious disabilities. If a person who's deaf is thought to be less intelligent, that's an example of ability bias. Brienna knows that firsthand.

Brienna's Story

Brienna, 15, gets good grades, loves running track, and doing artwork. Brienna is also deaf. She doesn't consider her deafness a disability, but she has encountered bias.

"I was the only deaf person that many people had met," the Wisconsin teen says of her mainstream high school. "I had to prove myself. I had to prove that I wasn't handicapped."

Brienna also had to set people straight about some misconceptions about deafness. "Some are so silly I can't believe they exist," she says. One kid told her that if she can sneeze, she isn't deaf. Someone else thought deaf people have no ears. Then there are people who yell when they try to communicate with her. "They think that if they just speak louder, I'll miraculously understand them. Honestly!" Brienna exclaims.

Other misconceptions are more serious, though. Brienna communicated through a translator who attended classes with her. Translation takes time, and some people would assume that meant Brienna was a slow thinker.

Brienna also felt like an outsider. "I always felt out of place," she says. "I felt singled out as the lone deaf."

That feeling of exclusion made Brienna decide to change schools. She now attends a school that is bilingual in American Sign Language and English, just like Brienna. She's excited that all her fellow students speak sign language. "I can actually joke with anyone I want to!" says Brienna.

"He's always been an outsider."

Aaron's Story

Aaron, 18, has a host of different challenges: Asperger's syndrome, obsessive-compulsive disorder, stuttering, and seizure disorders. Ability bias has made school extremely difficult for the Connecticut teen.

His mother recalled a characteristic event: "He was drawing something. Another kid came by and crumpled it up and put it in the trash. He came home from school that day and said, 'Everything I do is trash.' This is the way he was treated, the way he expected to be treated. He's always been an outsider."

Things began to change for Aaron when he joined a special theater group called the Unified Theater. It brings together typical kids and special kids, like Aaron, in an atmosphere of equality. Aaron has written and performed skits. He got to experience the thrill of the audience clapping for him and laughing at his jokes. "It felt great!" he says.

Kristen's Story

The color of Kristen's fourth-grade reading book was red. Her classmates had higher-level orange ones. The teacher also made Kristen sit in the back of the classroom. "I felt very excluded and alone, like I was being punished," Kristen recalls. "Kids would ridicule me and say things like 'Why do you have to sit in the back of the class?' Or 'What are you, stupid?' After a while I started wondering, 'Maybe they're right.'"

Kristen has dyslexia, a reading disability. Dyslexics sometimes fall behind their classmates in their studies. Sometimes they lash out in frustration or just give up. "I had this terrible insecurity that I didn't measure up," Kristen says. "I had a very poor self-image."

Bias #8: Appearance

How do I look? It's a question most teens ask themselves every day. In many ways, our society is obsessed with appearance. But what does a person's appearance really tell you about him? Not much. Appearance bias happens if you shun people you don't consider attractive. It also happens if you tease someone who is overweight—or if you make fun of someone who isn't wearing the "right" clothes. Appearance bias is extremely common in middle schools and high schools.

Steven's Story

Steven* is in eighth grade and lives in Long Island, New York. He sees appearance bias playing a big role in his school, especially for boys who are short and girls who are overweight. He also gets teased about his size.

I'm a big kid, and I get teased all the time. Kids will make elephant noises behind me. If I sit down, kids will say, "Oh, don't go break the chair now!" I don't eat a lot in school. I'm embarrassed to eat in front of the other kids. I don't want to get changed in front of kids for gym. It's so embarrassing. Kids don't care what they say. I don't want to go to gym in general. I know I'm slow and when we have to run the mile, kids shout, "Earthquuuuuake!" It's devastating.

*This student's name has been changed.

Chessi's Story

Chessi, 15, attends high school in Long Island, New York. She sees tremendous pressure on girls to look attractive and to be thin.

You're expected to act a certain way. Boys base their lives on ability—they get praise for being good at something. Girls base their lives on image—they get praise for being skinny and pretty. It's a big thing. Appearance is definitely what gets noticed for girls.

If a guy talks about a guy, it's going to be about what he's doing. If a guy talks about a girl, it's going to be about how hot she is.

Every girl in the world would want to be the epitome of beauty. But, for me, I think I'm more focused on things that are going to take me somewhere—like academics, music, writing— because that's how I'm going to make a living and how I'm going to be successful.

Bias #9: Social Class

According to some people, there are three social classes in the United States—the rich, the middle class, and the poor. And many teachers say that class differences are the number-one factor that divides students in their schools. Of course, no one can help what kind of family she was born into, but that doesn't stop some people from having a bias against people in other social classes.

Giancarlo's Story

Born in the Dominican Republic, Giancarlo came to the United States with his parents when he was a baby. For a while, both his parents, who are now divorced, worked. Now, though, both are unemployed. Giancarlo says he worries about every cent his family spends. "We're really scratching to get by," he says.

When he was younger, Giancarlo didn't really notice he was poor. "I was in a neighborhood where everyone was from the same background I was," he says. But now he goes to school with lots of wealthy kids.

There are definitely awkward moments. Friends will ask him to join them on expensive outings. "I'll joke around and say, 'You know I can't afford that,'" he says.

Still, Giancarlo's goal isn't to become a millionaire. "I just want to go on to better things and to write my own chapter," he says.

Massawa's Story

Massawa grew up in a housing project in the Bronx, a borough in New York City. Her mother, who raised her, suffers from a chronic illness and has not worked for five years.

"When I was younger, I didn't know I was poor," Massawa says. Then, when she was in junior high, some expensive boots changed that. "I wanted a pair because everyone was wearing them and I didn't want to be left out," Massawa says.

She told her mom, and for Christmas, she received a pair of a cheaper brand of boots. They were much less prestigious. "In my neighborhood," Massawa says, "you were ridiculed if you had [the cheaper] boots." It was a wake-up call. "I realized things like that do matter. It made me sad."

Massawa's goal is to lift her family out of poverty by becoming a lawyer. "I'm going to work ten times harder than the financially stable or rich kids do," she says. "I just really want to help people, and I'd like to be able to change the scenery for my mom and the rest of my family."

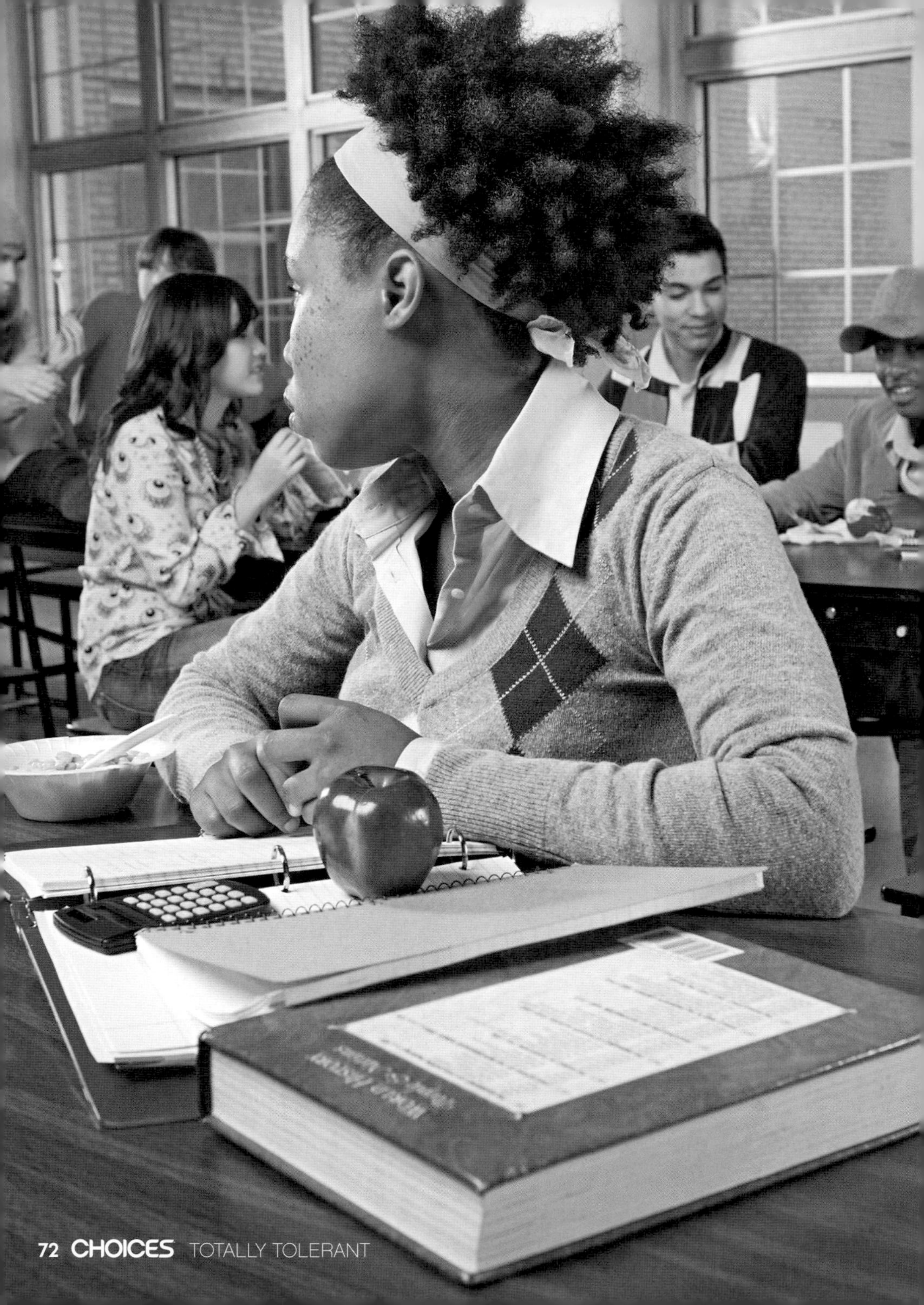

JOURNAL**IT!**

Write about a time you witnessed bias in your school. You can write about something that happened to you or write about what you've observed.

i'm not biased!

WHERE OUR BIASES COME FROM

Sorry, but you probably are biased. Everyone is in some way. If you've read this far, you know the harm that bias, prejudice, and intolerance can do. It hurts individuals, who find themselves excluded and judged. And whole communities are hurt when intolerance pits one group against another. But where do our biases come from? Understanding the answer to this question can help us fight the dangerous effects of intolerance.

Bias and Your Brain

Scientists are making great strides in understanding how our brains work and why we are all prone to having hidden biases. Consider this experiment, which was described in *Scientific American*. People were shown a short video of people playing basketball. They were asked to count how many times the ball was passed. At the end of the video, they shouted out their answers. Some said it was six times; others said nine. However, when asked to recall other details of the scene, everyone had missed something huge: they hadn't noticed a woman with an open white umbrella walking across the screen. They saw her only after they were told about her and watched the video a second time.

Our BRAINS ARE WIRED **to seek out the** IMPORTANT **information—and to screen out the details that don't seem to fit.**

Why do people miss the woman with the umbrella? Our brains are wired to seek out the important information—in this case the passing of the ball—and to screen out the details that don't seem to fit. "It's reasonable and rational," says Mahzarin Banaji, one of the researchers. "And it's an error."

And in everyday life, this error can lead to the kinds of intolerance teens described in Chapter Three. If you expect all the Asian kids you meet to be good at math, you might "screen out" the Asian kids who prefer sports to homework. This type of error keeps us from seeing people as they truly are. Instead, we only see what we expect to see.

test
YOURSELF ONLINE

Professor Banaji, along with her colleagues Anthony Greenwald and Brian Nosek, created an online experiment to test for hidden bias. It is called Project Implicit. (Something is implicit when it is sensed but not directly stated.) More than two million people have taken the tests online at https://implicit.harvard.edu/implicit/research.

The tests ask you to click on one picture or another as you are shown certain positive or negative words. The computer times how long it takes you to make these associations. The data has shown that most people, even those who say they are not biased, have preferences for people of their own race, gender, and culture. You can take the test, too. Maybe your generation will be the one to change this trend and get rid of hidden bias.

Bias and Your "In" Group

Scientists have seen that children as young as three years old can distinguish between "in groups" and "out groups." Preschoolers show preferences for their own families and their own school class members. When you think about it, this makes sense. A small child is completely dependent on his family for protection and survival. He needs to stick with his familiar group in order to be safe.

But what if a child's family members have some biased attitudes, or even worse, hateful prejudices? That child will learn intolerance and hate as if it were a natural, inevitable part of the world. "This allows [hate] to reproduce itself generation after generation," writes author Rush W. Dozier Jr. in his book, *Why We Hate*. "Hate is the nuclear weapon of the mind."

"Hate is the nuclear weapon of the mind."

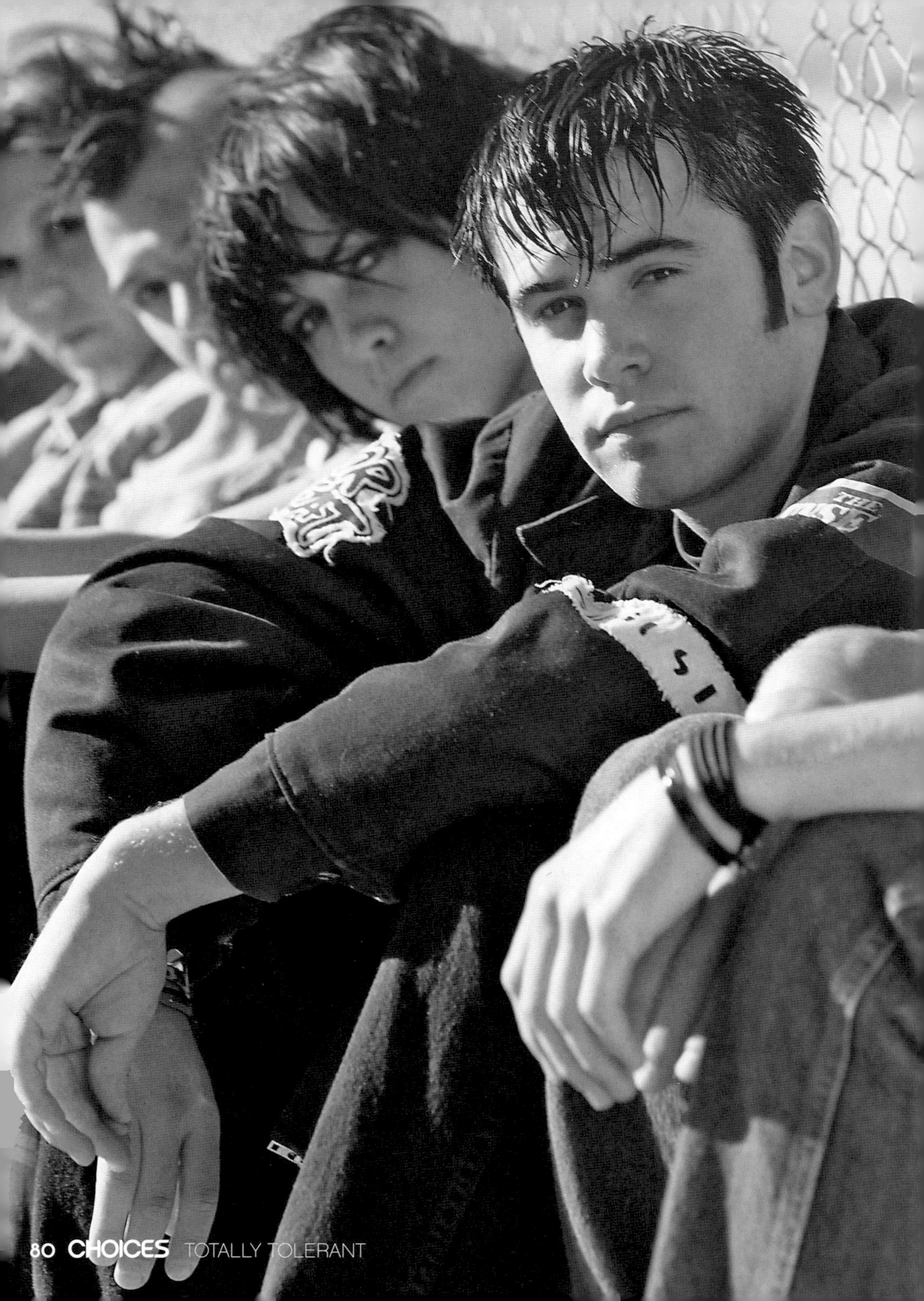

Dozier points out that we have a tendency to fall back on several either/or choices: us/them, friend/enemy, superior/inferior. "The superior/inferior classification, in particular, is central to most forms of prejudice," he writes.

These either/or distinctions have a biological basis. Our nervous systems want to immediately decide whether something is dangerous or not. We share this instinct with the rest of the animal world. Lots of animals, including humans, have an inborn fear of snakes, for example. Most of us don't wait to consider whether a snake is a harmless garter snake or a deadly rattlesnake. We jump back automatically when we see something slithering through the grass—just as a dog or a chimpanzee would.

But unlike those other animals, humans also have rational thought. And this is a kind of "override" system for those instinctual fears. A person who learns a lot about snakes wouldn't necessarily jump back at the sight of a garter snake. That person's conscious, rational thoughts can control the emotional, irrational fear response.

How does this work for people and in-groups and out-groups? Dozier argues that we can use rational thought to overcome our fears of "them" and develop our sense of empathy. Empathy is the ability to understand and identify with another person's feelings. Instead of viewing the world as "us/them," we can think about it as "us/us," emphasizing all the things we have in common with other people, even those who are culturally different from us. "Shifting from us/them to us/us will not end all conflict," Dozier writes. "But it will tend to minimize it."

A person can develop empathy and overcome hidden biases, even if her family and friends holds those biases. It takes some work, but it is possible. (Read more about overcoming bias in Chapter Five.)

Bias and the Media

Professor Banaji notes that bias is "in the air" around us. How does it get there? One of the most important ways bias is transmitted is through the media. Once you are on the lookout for stereotypes in the media, you will see them all the time.

smart
TV
Think about these questions as you watch TV:

1. WHO is shown in commercials for household cleaning products? Men or women? Everyone knows that men do housework. So why are they rarely in commercials for these products?

2. WHO is most often shown in a fight or a battle scene? Men or women? Why are men more frequently cast in such violent roles?

3. CAN you think of any TV shows that have groups of friends of different races or ethnicities? There are a few, but why are racially mixed groups of friends so uncommon on TV?

Any one show or commercial doesn't necessarily breed prejudice. But when so many of them present the same picture, we begin to get certain messages. We learn: "Housework is women's work," "It's okay for men to be violent," and "All my friends should look like me." These are the kinds of attitudes that limit all of us.

ANALYZE it!

The next time you are watching TV, use these questions to analyze some commercials.

WHAT is the product being advertised?

WHAT is the gender, race, and age (child, teen, or adult) of the main character in the commercial?

WHO is meant to buy this product?

WHAT kinds of people are excluded from the message?

CAN you identify any stereotypes that the advertisers are using?

When you start thinking critically about the advertisements you see, you will begin to identify the hidden biases in them.

bias busting

bias busting

WHAT YOU CAN DO TO BECOME TOTALLY TOLERANT

We can't undo the damage intolerance has caused in the past. But what about the future? Each one of us has the power to make a difference in our society. This chapter is about what teens can do to build a welcoming, fair, and totally tolerant future.

Pay Attention to What You Say

One of the places bias creeps into our daily lives is in our language. Name-calling and teasing just aren't funny. Before you make fun of one of your friends or someone you don't know very well, think about how it would feel to trade places with her. Can you honestly expect her to laugh when you're making her the punch line of a joke?

There is one phrase that is rampant in middle schools and high schools today: "That's so gay!" How many times a day do you hear someone say that phrase? Maybe you've even said it yourself. Teens say that they use the word *gay* to stand in for lots of other negative words (such as *stupid* or *disgusting*). You would never hear a friend say, "Wow, I love your sneakers. They are so gay!"

In a moment of frustration, you might blurt out, "This book is soooo gay!" If you really meant to say that you don't like the book, why not say that? Did you *really* mean to put down a whole group of people to express a negative opinion about a book?

When a person uses the word *gay* in this negative way, chances are that someone else feels offended or put down. In a 2002 *Teen People* poll of 7,818 teens, 22 percent identified themselves as gay, lesbian, bisexual, transgender, or questioning of their sexual orientation. That is a lot of teens. And they are getting hurt when people who are "just kidding" say, "That's so gay!"

Eradicate Insults

Sometimes the bias in our language is even more direct. Words such as *faggot*, *lame*, and *retard* are hurled at people. Sometimes the targets are gay or disabled or mentally challenged people; sometimes they aren't. These words are almost always fueled by aggression and are clearly meant to be insulting and humiliating.

If you witness this kind of bias, you can question it. Ask, "What do you *really* mean by that, anyway?" Sometimes, just questioning people about their language will make them realize that what they are saying is inappropriate.

The GET.A.VOICE PROJECT challenges teens to use their voices in positive ways. The project, which is now in 15 schools in Long Island, New York, asks students to take an oath to think about their words and to stand up for others when they hear disrespectful language. The motto is: "Be a leader. Make a difference. Get a voice."

FIND YOUR VOICE

Get.A.Voice students learn that words are powerful. They can really change the way people think and feel—in good ways or bad ways. Students practice strategies for dealing with negative language. When someone says something hurtful or disrespectful, they respond:

"That's really rude. Stop saying that!"

"If you're *just* kidding, JUST STOP!"

"Did you *really* mean that? Say what you mean."

Meanwhile, students learn to have a positive impact on their friends by noticing—and saying out loud—what they like about each other. Here are some sentence starters to get the positive vibes flowing:

"I like it when you . . . "

"Thanks for noticing . . . "

"I'm really glad . . . "

"I appreciate it when . . . "

"Thanks for . . . "

"That made me feel so . . . "

For information on how to bring the GET.A.VOICE PROJECT to your school, go to **www.getavoice.net.**

Get Active

To really get serious about stopping bias, you can find ways to become an activist. Here are some ideas.

Volunteer: You can expand your horizons and challenge any hidden biases you may have by volunteering to work for an organization that serves a community or population different than your own, such as recent immigrants or older adults. Or your school may have peer educator or peer moderator programs. If you volunteer for these, you will be trained to promote respect and conflict resolution (peaceful ways of resolving disputes) at your school.

Mix It Up: Each year, tolerance.org promotes Mix It Up at Lunch Day. The point of the day is to counteract the way that most teens segregate themselves during lunch. On this day, schools find ways to make sure that teens get outside of their comfort zones and socialize with people who are not necessarily like themselves.

Schools accomplish this in different ways. Some schools give out colored bracelets. People with orange bracelets sit at orange lunch tables, red bracelets at red tables. Another school labels lunch tables by months. People with June birthdays sit at the June table, probably with people they don't know well. At other schools, students were given pieces of paper with one letter on it. The students then had to find others with different letters to spell out the words M-I-X I-T U-P. To learn more about Mix It Up at Lunch Day, go to www.tolerance.org/teens.

You can apply for a grant from tolerance.org to help bring down the walls that divide your school. Shira Beery used a $500 grant to start a Diversity Week at her school, Stuyvesant High School in New York City. The grant allowed her to bring in speakers and organize workshops and film screenings.

Attend meetings of the Gay-Straight Alliance at your high school. This student organization works to provide a safe and supportive environment for lesbian, gay, bisexual, and transgender youth and their straight allies. If your school doesn't have this organization, look into forming one.

Help Your School

Does your school have an explicit respect policy? If it doesn't, you may want to talk to a teacher or administrator about looking at what other schools have done. Having a policy that everyone can read, understand, and put into practice can help your school become a place where tolerance is the norm. This is the Respect Policy that was created at Mariner High School in Everett, Washington:

RESPECT is the cornerstone of all our interactions and behaviors. We acknowledge the dignity and worth of one another and strive never to diminish another by our conduct or our attitudes.

Associate principal Paula Martin and her colleagues spent months developing the policy to help students in the very diverse school get along better. Later, all the schools in Mukilteo, Washington, adopted it. Students talk about the policy in small groups, and everyone at the school has a responsibility to live by it.

ACTIONSTEPS

Here are the action steps to take when you see disrespect.

STEP ONE: When you witness behavior that is in violation of the Respect Policy, tell the person to stop. Apathy, silence, or laughter encourages the abuse and further disrespects the victims. Inform an adult in school and your parents.

STEP TWO: If the behavior doesn't stop, contact an administrator as soon as possible to initiate a complaint.

STEP THREE: If the behavior continues, keep a journal of further incidents, including description, time, date, place, and witnesses. Keep your parents and administrators informed.

Teen Voices

How can teens make themselves and their communities totally tolerant? Here are some of the action statements students came up with at one junior high school. The school celebrated Martin Luther King Jr. Day with speakers, workshops, and performances. At the end of the day, they were all asked to reflect on what they could do to change. Here's how students finished the sentence that began: *After thinking about today's events, I will make a conscious decision to . . .*

Try and hold back some racist slurs that are jokes but could offend others. After all, our words mean more than we realize.
—Kristen, 8th grade

Respect people who are different than myself.
—Rachel, 8th grade

Not laugh at others because everyone else is laughing.
—Christa, 9th grade

Not make fun of people because I wouldn't want to have that done to me.
—Kate, 7th grade

Be more interested in other cultures aside from mine. Today's events proved to me how interesting African culture is. It has inspired me to start to learn about other cultures.
—*Jessica, 7th grade*

Help all of my friends to stand up for themselves and enlist aid.
—*Annette, 8th grade*

Be more respectful of other people. Being exposed to openly gay people made me more aware about the troubled and difficult encounters they are forced to experience.
—*George, 9th grade*

Be nice to people not like me.
—*David, 9th grade*

Not expect someone to be smart or stupid based on their looks, hair color, skin color, or where they are from. To just treat people the way they should be treated.

—*Elizabeth, 8th grade*

Learn to not accept hurtful things that hateful, ignorant, mean people dish out. I want to learn to speak up, yet I also want to know when to keep my mouth shut.

—*Paul, 7th grade*

Do whatever is in my power to stop prejudice against every race. I'm going to do this because I realize that [people of every] age, race, color, religion, or culture have something good to offer to the world.

—*Kim, 7th grade*

Try to contribute to this world by exposing myself to different ethnic groups and races.

—*Karen, 8th grade*

Totally Tolerant

Those students have the right idea. They are changing themselves first, and this is the most important thing any of us can do. This is the path to a totally tolerant society—the path to acceptance, respect, and inclusion.

You can

Follow the lead of these kids and find ways to bring more tolerance to your community.

bias—a prejudice or preconceived opinion about something or someone. A bias implies an unfavorable judgment.

discrimination—treating someone unfairly or unjustly because of their class, race, or other category rather than by who they are as individuals

diversity—the quality of having different characteristics; the coming together of people from various, diverse backgrounds

demeaning—insulting or damaging to another's character

ethnicity—a way human beings identify with or are members of a particular racial, national, or cultural group that has distinct customs, beliefs, or languages

hate crime—a crime motivated by bias against an individual because of his or her race, religion, sexual orientation, disability, ethnicity, nationality, age, gender, gender identity, or political affiliation; also known as a bias crime

homogeneous—all the same

intolerance—lack of tolerance or respect for persons of different races or backgrounds

prejudice—a negative opinion about a person or group, formed without sufficient knowledge

racism—the belief that one race is superior to another

sexist—behavior that displays discrimination or hatred against people based on their gender rather than their individual merits; the belief that one gender is superior to or more valuable than the other

sexual orientation—one's natural physical attraction to people of the opposite sex (heterosexuality), the same sex (homosexuality), or both (bisexuality)

stereotypes—usually negative ideas about members of particular groups based on a generalization of characteristics

tolerance—the ability to respect individuals or groups who may be disapproved of by those in the majority

totally

Books

Abrahams, George. *Boy v. Girl? How Gender Shapes Who We Are, What We Want, and How We Get Along.* Minneapolis: Free Spirit, 2002.

Desetta, Al. *The Courage to Be Yourself: True Stories by Teens About Cliques, Conflicts, and Overcoming Peer Pressure.* Minneapolis: Free Spirit and Educators for Social Responsibility, 2005.

Dozier, Rush W. *Why We Hate: Understanding, Curbing, and Eliminating Hate in Ourselves and Our World.* Chicago: Contemporary Books, McGraw-Hill, 2002.

Gaskins, Pearl Fuyo. *What Are You? Voices of Mixed-Race Young People.* New York: Henry Holt and Company, 1999.

Mandel, Laurie. *Teen Girls Get a Voice: Writing, Rapping, and Taking Action!* New York: ActionWorks, Inc. (available at www. getavoice.net/getavoicebook.html)

Smith, David J. *If the World Were a Village: A Book about the World's People.* Toronto: Kids Can Press, 2002.

Online Sites & Organizations

Gay Straight Alliance

www.gaystraightalliance.org
This student organization works to provide a safe and supportive environment for lesbian, gay, bisexual, and transgender youth and their straight allies.

Get.A.Voice Project

www.getavoice.net
Log on to this Web site and read about how other teens are empowered to use their voices to speak up against name-calling and bullying in their schools. Take the Get.A.Voice survey, check out how kids are making a difference in their schools, or write to share how you're using your voice to be a leader and create change in your community!

Learning from a Legacy of Hate

www.bsu.edu/learningfromhate/default.htm
This Web site was started by 15 college students at Ball State University in Indiana to educate about hate speech and to open people's minds and hearts to the experiences of others. Click on the map of Indiana to watch videos and hear recordings of students and others who have dealt with bias crimes.

Mix It Up

tolerance.org
Take a look at how other students have "mixed it up" at their schools, and how you can help break the walls of intolerance in your school and community. Mix It Up is a project of the Teaching Tolerance program.

Judaism, 39, 46

K

"Karen," 101
"Karlee," 53–54
"Kate," 99
"Kevin," 47–49
"Kim," 101
"Kristen," 66, 99

L

"Lana," 56
language bias, 35, 38, 90–91, 92, 93
laws, 36, 38, 39, 43
lesbians, 52, 53–54, 91, 95
lynchings, 22, 28

M

Mariner High School (Washington), 96–97
Martin Luther King Jr. Day, 99
Martin, Paula, 97
"Massawa," 71
media bias, 83, 85, 86
men, 56, 85, 86
Mix It Up at Lunch Day, 94–95
"Molly," 8–9, 12, 33, 60
Muslims. *See* Islamic religion.

N

NAACP (National Association for the Advancement of Colored People), 35
Native Americans, 18–19, 27, 43
Nazi Party, 39, 46
negative language, 35, 90–91, 92, 93
neo-Nazi hate groups, 46
nooses, 22, 24, 28, 31, 36
Nosek, Brian, 78
"n-word," 35

O

obsessive-compulsive disorder, 65

P

"Paul," 101
perspective, 13
poverty, 70, 71
prejudice. *See* bias.
Project Implicit, 78

R

"Rachel," 99
racism, 31, 32, 42–43, 44, 45
Ramadan (Islamic holy month), 8–9
rational thought, 82
religion
    Christianity, 8
    Christmas holiday, 8
    Eid al-Fitr (Ramadan feast), 9
    fasting, 8–9, 12
    Islamic religion, 8, 12, 46
    Judaism, 39, 46
    Ramadan (Islamic holy month), 8–9
    Sikhism, 47–49
religious bias, 46, 47–49
respect
    definition of, 12, 13
    diversity and, 12
    intolerance and, 32
    policies, 96–97
    showing, 15
    tolerance and, 9, 16, 19
    volunteering and, 94

S

Scientific American magazine, 76–77
seizure disorders, 65
September 11 attacks, 46

About the Authors

Laurie Mandel is an artist, activist, researcher, and educator at Murphy Junior High School in Stony Brook, New York. She is the founder of the Get.A.Voice Project, an education program to address name-calling through leadership and youth empowerment. Mandel has written a book with teens entitled *Teen Girls Get a Voice*; has had students featured on National Public Radio; and won the Myra Sadker Curriculum Award at American University for her work on gender issues in middle school.

Diane Webber is an author and editor who has written five nonfiction books for teens. "I really love hearing what teens have to say," she says. "I hope my books represent teen voices well and help teens learn from each other." *Totally Tolerant* is Webber's first experience working with a co-author. "I have tremendous admiration for the work Laurie has done to change the culture of her school to one of respect," she says. "I hope this book shows how teens everywhere have the power to do the same thing." Webber lives in the Washington, D.C., area with her husband and twin sons.

Acknowledgments

The authors thank Kim Ciano for her contribution to this book. We also thank the students who shared their very important, valuable experiences with us.